WHAT REMAINS OF MY HEART

ALEXIS M ROMO

Copyright © 2021
Alexis M Romo

"What Remains Of My Heart"

All rights reserved. No part of this publication may
be reproduced, distributed or conveyed without
the permission of the author.

This is for every hopeless romantic out there:
every person who gives so much to the ones they love,
and all those who know that true love is out there waiting for them ...

including myself.

A PERSONAL BOOK COLLECTION/GRAVEYARD OF PAST LOVES

One day, every person that I have ever loved

will have a book written about them,

each one with our story and memories together

etched into the pages that will remain forever,

like tombstones,

because even though our love may have died,

my memory of them never will.

THE LOVES THAT REMAIN

My love for my exes,

my crushes,

people I never got a chance to be with,

and even those random strangers

I temporarily fell in love with as I walked by,

will forever remain in my heart

because even though

they may not be in my life anymore,

they remain in mine,

even if they're only just a memory or a dream,

even if I never got to be with them

in this lifetime ...

HOPELESS ROMANTIC

How many of you

identify as a hopeless romantic?

You're a sucker

for love letters,

romantic poems,

small gestures

that lets the person know

that they are loved and cared for deeply?

But do you know what the keyword is there?

Sucker.

We're suckers.

We're suckers

if we believe that a romantic partner

will show their care

and devotion and love

with flowers,

chocolates,

or even a small note

that reminds you

that you are the light of their life.

We're suckers

if we believe in fairy-tale romances

that we've only ever really seen

on the movie screen

and we lowkey know that

that type of romance is impossible

but we still believe in it anyway.

We're suckers

if we believe that true love exists,

that we have a soulmate

somewhere in this world

and that we are destined to find them

and be with them.

We're suckers

if we believe in monogamous relationships

and that we want to commit to them

with our partner,

and believe that there are people capable of not cheating or

betraying you.

We're suckers

if we believe that true love conquers all,

and that nothing

could ever stand in the way of it

despite obstacles

and struggles
and tribulations.

We're suckers
if we believe that love isn't a lie,
that love is something that takes time to find
and that it is patient and kind
but is worth waiting for in the end.

Us hopeless romantics,

we're suckers for believing in love.

We really are ...

But guess what?

I'd rather be an optimistic sucker
than a heartless pessimist.

I'd rather believe in love
than not believe in it at all.

LITTLE THINGS BY @SPARKILING._.LAVENDER (INSTAGRAM)

Love is in the little things:

it isn't always vocally audible.

You find it in their small gestures,

gratitude,

and care.

These are all, in fact,

acts of love that are just for you.

The soothing touch whenever you feel blue,

the quality time you spend together,

the feeling of, *"You're mine forever."*

Great loves aren't audible — they are hidden,

in little things which you see.

The sense of knowing that, when no one else is,

we'll still be together,

you and me.

SUPERNOVA

I want fireworks

and I want electricity

and I want the stars to sparkle,

no,

I want them to explode

and burst with light –

I want supernovas

every time we kiss

so the rest of the world knows

that there's a love that burns so bright

that it can light up

each dark space of the universe

UNIVERSE

You look at me

like the universe is being born

right in front of you ...

PRAYING FOR YOU

All I wanna do

is write you love notes

and tell you everything

about your heart and soul

that makes me fall to my knees,

praying to God

that He allows me to keep you

in my life forever ...

A MILLION LOVE POEMS

Got a million love poems in my head

and all of them are for you ...

A DREAM

You make me sound like a dream

with each poem you write about me.

You make me sound like a goddess

walking among the earth,

like an angel,

with wings undamaged

and with my halo

still crowned perfectly upon my head,

that has descended

from the holy staircase

that leads to Heaven.

You make my most mundane features

sound like they are rare jewels

or newly discovered

natural wonders of the world.

You see my eyes as pools of honey

and my skin as sweet white mocha chocolate

and you see my smile as a sparkle

that no star could ever match,

one that the moon

would want to always be close to in the night.

You make me sound like a dream,

one that anyone would fall in love with.

You make me sound like the girl

that someone would fall in love with

at first sight,
like I am Juliet,
and you make me sound like a girl
capable of turning anyone
into a nervous wreck in the presence of me,
or into a fool who stumbles with their words
trying to find just the right ones to say.

You make me sound like a dream,
in every poem you write about me
and I hope that someday
I can fall in love with myself
the way you have fallen in love with me.

REINCARNATED LOVE

I'm not sure if I believe in reincarnation

and lifetimes that have come before

and ones that will come after this one

but if I learn one day that I get to be reborn

and have another chance to try life again,

I want to be able to find you

in each lifetime that comes after this one

and fall in love with you all over again ...

MY LOVE LANGUAGE

My primary love language is words of affirmation

that means I need to hear my partner tell me

that they love me

and that I am the most beautiful soul

in the world to them.

I need to hear every sweet nothing

pour out of their lips

and I need to read text messages

adorned with heart emojis and smiley faces.

And I need my partner to talk about me to

to their friends and family

and tell them that I am absolutely

the most amazing person they have ever known

and I want to hear their friends tell me:

"they talk about you all the time"

and I want to hear their family say:

"you're perfect for them –

you are just what they need."

And I want my significant other to leave me

little love notes on the kitchen counter

next to my keys

and a freshly prepared cup of coffee

that says things like:

"have a beautiful day"

or *"can't wait for our date tonight."*

I want love notes and poems,

handwritten by my partner,

illustrating their love for me in words

written in black,

engraved on every color of paper.

I want my partner to send me

their favorite love songs

with lyrics that resemble their love for me

and everything they want to say

and they couldn't have said it better.

My love language is words of affirmation.

I'd like to think that I know

true love when I hear it,

when I see the scribbles of words on the page

or the clearly written ones on the screen.

But the truth is, because I am a writer,

I always try to find the meaning in words

because I always aim to put meaning into mine.

FALL FOR WORDS

Maybe I'm a sucker
because I fall in love with words

and not actions.

And why wouldn't I fall for words?

I am a writer, after all.

My whole existence
revolves around my passion for words
and how stringed together
in just the right way,
they can light up my entire day.

IS LOVE WORTH IT?

I hold out so much hope for love,

and why shouldn't I?

If there is one thing to hope for in this world,

one thing to desire,

it should be love:

pure,

raw,

and irrevocable love.

But I do wonder

if love is something I should chase and pursue

or if it is something I must wait patiently for,

because I have the tendency

to chase those who are not worthy of my heart

but I also tend to grow impatient quickly.

Are my efforts required

or am I enough to stand alone

and wait for love to come to me?

Are you waiting for me to make the first move

or am I waiting for you?

Is love worth waiting for

or is it worth fighting for?

CAN'T FALL FOR YOU

I can't let myself fall for someone

who doesn't exist

I can't let myself fall for someone

who's only a figment of my imagination,

who is merely the false scenarios

and made up of my daydreams.

I can't let myself fall for someone

who's only truth

is that their physical person actually exists

in this time and space,

but their love and affection for me

is something that only my imagination

or a fairy tale could possibly conjure up.

I can't let myself fall for someone

who is blinded

by their own ego

and who is only motivated

by the sight of a pretty girl walking by

and is easily distracted by her body

and her smile

and her flirty wink.

I can't let myself fall for someone who promises

that his intentions for me are true

and that his eyes are only fixated on me

but fucks any girl who comes
within his line of sight.

I can't let myself fall for someone like you ...

... not again

BREAK MY HEART

I'm so madly in love with you -
I don't care if you hurt me ....

I'd be honored to have my heart broken by you,
piece by piece ....

BREAK MY HEART

I'm so madly in love with you -
I don't care if you hurt me ....

LOVELORN

Woe is the lovelorn soul,

the poor thing

that tears itself in pieces
and rips itself apart at the seams
all for the name of love

only to learn that they're left
with the fragments and remains
of what they gave away,
that the one they love
won't ever put back together for them
because they never wanted them
in the first place ...

BAD GUY

Heartbreaks are easier

when the person cheated on you

or simply had too many red flags

for you to ignore any longer

because you can hate them,

you have reason to hate them –

it makes the pain understandable

and you learn how to not need them

because you know that

they never truly loved you.

You

were never the bad guy –

but it's easier to paint you as one.

After we ended things,

I looked for all that weird stuff,

whatever was bad or wrong

or hiding in you

to make the pain of my heart

easier to bear and quicker to move on.

But you were never the bad guy –

you loved me

the way I always wanted to be loved

and the way I thought I deserved.

But even my love was not enough
for the man who loved me
with every bit of his heart …

I know that deep down, I am enough,

but I'm painting you as the bad guy,
remember?

I have to pretend like I'm not enough
in order for me to move on …

STAR-CROSSED

My heart still hurts

the pain you've caused me

is unmatched

because we loved each other

with every bit of our souls

but our relationship was futile

and doomed from the start

Star-crossed lovers, we were,

like Romeo and Juliet

the stars may have brought us together

but we created supernovas in each other

and if we were together any longer,

we would've exploded to stardust -

we would've been specks

floating in the universe

with no chance

of ever coming together again

but I anxiously await the day

we reunite

because we can still have a happy ending

even if we are no longer

star-crossed lovers.

We can still have a happy ending –

maybe all we need is a new beginning

<u>WHEN I MISS YOU THE MOST</u>

It's such a cliché, isn't it –
to say that I miss you in lonely moments?

I do miss you
on the nights without you:
the nights when you are spending time
with your friends,
the business trips,
and the holidays spent without you …

but it's the moments when I'm enjoying
an iced chai latte
while I'm basking in the warm sun,
book in hand
and pen in the other
and I'm highlighting all the parts
I'm falling in love with as I go along

and it's the moments when the music is loud
but everyone is dancing
and everyone is laughing
and time passes and for once,
we aren't worried about it ticking by
and we're simply enjoying life,
realizing that this is what it's meant to be

and it's the moments when joy is at its peak
and I am free of my worries
and all I want is to share it with you

those are the moments
when I miss you the most ...

HOW OFTEN AM I ON YOUR MIND?

I still dream of you,

despite the many months that have passed,

and I'm sure you've dreamt of me,

but how long does my image last?

Am I merely a passing thought

that occasionally crosses through?

Or am I ever-present in your head?

Does my image always stay with you?

You never leave my thoughts,

for you're forever etched in my heart.

But I know that the stitches of your memory

can't keep it from falling apart.

Despite the heartache I've experienced,

I still hold out hope for love,

and I hold out for rainbows and sunlight,

and for answered prayers and doves.

I know I can't wait for you forever

but there's no doubt we'll reunite in time –

we'll be together again, maybe not now,

but maybe in some other lifetime.

RUNAWAY

You wanted my love

from the beginning -

you waited,

patiently,

for it.

You waited for years,

and I apologize

for making you wait so long,

but once I was ready

to hand you every bit of my love,

you ran away

like a coward -

my love was too much for you,

you were too afraid to let me love you

but I'm still trying to understand why:

why would you,

or anyone,

run away from a love

they've been waiting for?

OPTIMISM

You say that optimism

is what makes me who I am –

my can-do attitude,

coupled with a never-ending faith

that good things will come

and that things are working exactly

the way they are meant to.

You made me lose that optimism.

You see,

I was optimistic

when I decided to sit down

at the same table as you

the day we met in our literature class.

I was optimistic

when I agreed to hang out with you

outside of class for the first time,

discussing poetry and exchanging

bits of information about each other.

I was optimistic

when I said yes

and we had our first date at your apartment

where you made me dinner

and you danced with me.

I was optimistic

when you said you would always be there for me,

despite the many times I was too afraid

to let you in so close to my heart

and to my damaged soul.

I was optimistic

when I finally fell in love with you

because I knew that you loved me

with every bit of your heart

and I believed that love conquers all.

I was always optimistic

when it came to you,

even in moments I was scared –

I still held onto that faith, that hope,

that things were going the way they were meant to.

But here I am:

heartbroken

and too broken to have optimism

when it comes to you.

Maybe that's just karma.

I've hurt you,
I hurt you first.

Maybe I deserve this.
Maybe I don't deserve optimism
when it comes to love,
when it comes to matters of the heart.

YOU LOVED ME

My dad had sent me something saying that
you need to stick with the guy who loves you
and not the guy you love.
This is because the guy who loves you
will always do whatever it takes to be with you
but the guy you love
will only love you when it's on his terms.

You loved me.
You loved me first.
You loved me wholeheartedly.

But once I fell in love with you,
the love you once had for me was gone.
You claimed it was still there
and that it would always be there,
but that wasn't true, was it?
Because if it was there,
you would still be here with me.

You would be doing whatever it takes
to be with me.

But here I am,
alone,
loving a guy
that only loves me on his terms.

SET ME FREE

My golden heart has turned to stone

but what can I do?

People chipped too much away from me

and now I try to take the remains

and turn it into a masterpiece,

for no one else,

but only for me.

My wings are heavy and they are so weak

but what can I say?

It sure hurt like Hell when I fell from Heaven

and now I'm stuck on Earth

and I'm not even sure

if I'm an angel anymore,

for my angelic radiance has dimmed,

but the light is still burning softly.

I'm weighed down by the chains

but who can set me free?

I keep gazing at you

and hope that you can set me free,

and for us to trade keys,

for I want you to see what is behind my door

but it is only I who can open the cage door

SILENT TREATMENT

I hate that you don't talk to me anymore.

We had so much history. So many secrets exchanged. Words untold to anyone else besides each other. We've seen each other at our best and at our worst. We've seen each other's naked souls, vulnerably put on display. We've seen the inside of each other's hearts. You saw mine surrounded by a cage because I didn't want it be damaged anymore and I saw yours trying to stay away from the brightness, for you feared you weren't good enough for the light.

But now you won't even
conjure up a "hello" anymore.

You can't tell me that you miss me,
but I know that you do.

You can't tell me you love me anymore,
but I know you still do.

I hate that you don't talk to me anymore.

I hate it.

I hate it.

I hate it.

Why can't you talk to me anymore?

I'M ONLY HUMAN ...

I'm only human, you know,

and sometimes I miss you

and I wanna see how you're doing.

Sometimes I wanna text or call you

to see what you're currently pursuing.

Sometimes I want to see you

and I want to hang out like old times.

Sometimes I want to be friends again –

I just want my partner in crime.

I know that we can't erase the past,

which is such a pity and such a shame,

because even if we did hang out,

I know that it wouldn't be the same.

And sometimes I just want you to say my name

and tell me that you messed up back then.

And sometimes I want you to apologize

so we can move forward and be together again.

I'm only human, you know

and though all I want is a chance to make up,

I know that nothing will ever be the same

and that there is never again going to be an "us ..."

UNSENT LETTERS

I write letters to the ones I love
and to the ones I've lost.

Woe is my heart,
for it can pour
sweet nothings and everythings
onto the page
but can never say them aloud.

And worse yet,
my heart can pour
sweet nothings and everythings
onto the page
but does not have the courage
to ever send the letter.

THE LETTERS I WROTE BUT NEVER SENT: FOR R.N.

Dear R.N.,

I think it's strange that you were my first real boyfriend. Our middle school romance was predictable: it was never going to last. We were too young and stupid and naïve to believe that our relationship would ever survive. I didn't even have a thorough understanding of what it means to be in a relationship and to be in love. I just knew that I liked the idea of love. I liked the idea of Prince Charming and being rescued from all the woes that life throws at me. I liked the idea of having that one person who loves you forever. I liked the idea of being the one person who meant the most to someone. I liked the idea of you.

But you weren't what I thought you'd be. You weren't Prince Charming –you were never going to be him. But even though you weren't my knight-in-shining-armor that was going to rescue this damsel in distress, you still introduced me to this thing called "love." We were never in love - I think we just loved the idea of being in love.

But regardless of everything that's happened between us, whether it was true love or not, I will always reserve a special place in my heart just for you: my first love.

THE LETTERS I WROTE BUT NEVER SENT: FOR R.M.

Dear R.M.,

It's been too long since we've last spoken. And I don't mean that in a "I miss you and I still love you" kind of way, though it is true that I do. I do miss you. I miss our laughs, our memories, and our genuine moments of bliss. I miss you being a friend, even though we never were just friends. You were always more, at least to me. You were the man I thought I'd spend my life with (but who are we kidding – I knew deep down that we weren't meant to be).

And I do still love you, believe it or not. It's not that romantic love or head-over-heels-love ... The love I have for you is simply about memory and preserving that memory. You caused me a lot of pain and a lot of heartache for years. I honestly thought that that pain would never end. I thought I was doomed to be alone and live my life with that constant heartache. But I still love you. I love your confidence and your sense of humor. I love your smile and your ability to never be too serious. I love that you exist and that you were once an important part of my life. I love that you are now only a memory, even if it's a mostly painful one. I love you, as a fellow human being on this earth. I will always love you. I will always hold a special place in my heart for those who mean so much to me, even if it was in the past.

You've caused me too much pain for me to ever be romantically in love with you again. I still carry that pain, though it is not as heavy on my shoulders or my heart anymore. But despite this,

I do hope all is well with you. I don't expect you to miss or love me, but just know that I miss and love you. Always.

THE LETTERS I WROTE BUT NEVER SENT: FOR M.A.

Dear M.A.,

I've been wanting to tell you so much. It feels so strange not talking to you every day. I'm not upset with you – I understand both yours and my reasons for going our separate ways. It was for the best. But I do miss you every day. I've been reflecting a lot about you and us and what we were and what we are now and what we will be later on.

And the one thing that I keep going back to is the fact that you are the only person who has truly loved me. And I keep asking myself: "Why would he leave me if he truly does love me?" A part of me is still hurt and angry but even with the pain and anger I still carry, I don't hate you – I don't think I ever could. Even after heartbreak, I still believe in love and forgiveness. I still love even after relationships end. It may not be that intense, passionate, romantic love but there's still love and a wish for the person to be happy and well.

I wish the same for you: I wish for happiness and good fortune to be bestowed upon you. I wish love that is true for you. I wish for every dream of yours to come true. Why would I not wish these things for you? I still love you. I will always love you. You showed me what true love is. And I am forever indebted and grateful to you for that.

I guess all I'm really trying to say is that no matter what happens going forward, I hope you're happy, and that I miss you, and I hope we can be friends again someday. Though I'll admit that I'm probably stupid for even wanting to talk to you, when it comes to love, you gotta listen to your heart. And all my heart wants is to talk to you. To be friends with you. To have you in my life.

Anyway, I hope you're doing well and staying safe.

Until the next time we reconnect, with all my love.

LOVE IS (A) ...

FOREVER
YOU
DRUG
UNPREDICTABLE
SCARY
SACRED
SELF-
LESS
PAIN
FEELING
CHOICE
LIBERATING
HAPPINESS
SUFFERING
LOVE
PATIENT
HOME
KIND
PROMISE
BATTLEFIELD
ACCEPTANCE
SOUVENIR
FRUSTRATING
UNCONDITIONAL
LIGHT
VERB
EVERYTHING
POISION
COMPLICATED
WAR
DEAD
REAL
FORGIVING
MARATHON

DREAMING OF HAPPILY EVER AFTER

You claim that you want to dream of me forever,

and though that may be true,

I was real – I still am.

I am here in this time and space,

the same one you exist in, yet,

all you desire is to dream of me.

You only want me to be present in a place

where you can alter me, my image, my personality.

You can fix my flaws and erase my mistakes,

as well as yours.

In your dreams,

I am your personal Barbie doll,

and you can dress me up however you'd like

to fit whatever fantasy you have to fulfill.

In your dreams, you can paint yourself as the hero

and I am your damsel-in-distress,

locked away in the tower,

guarded by the fire-breathing dragon.

You can come in on your noble steed,

galloping valiantly to rescue me

from the cage you locked me in.

But we both know that in reality,

    you are a coward.

You are too afraid to love me,

too afraid to even allow me to love you.

You are no Prince Charming –

you're no prince at all.
You are not even the beast
who turns into the prince
with true love's first kiss.
And for the longest time,
I thought that I simply did not possess the magic
that turns beasts into princes.
But I've learned that princesses and queens
don't need that power anyway
because she is already whole and plenty
on her own.
And though I've dreamed of a fairytale romance,
you are no fairytale.
You are a chapter, though admittedly sometimes,
I wish you were only a mere paragraph.
But you are a chapter in my story,
as I am one in yours.

But I am both the princess
and the author of this tale
and it is up to me to create the happily ever after
I am destined to have.
I realized that you only want
to keep me in your dreams
because you are too afraid to pick up your pen
and include me in your happily ever after.
You are too afraid to write the ending you deserve.

BEAUTIFUL MESS

I once did a paper for a class in college about the meaning behind the painting called *"Mrs. Sarah Siddons as the Tragic Muse"* by Sir Joshua Reynolds done in the 17th century. I won't go into detail, but in this painting, Sarah Siddons was a lovely, beautiful woman filled with tragedy, chaos, and madness. And the more I've thought about this painting and analyzed it in my head over time, the more I realize that she is the embodiment of a "beautiful mess."

I, too, am a beautiful mess.

And the more I've thought about it and analyzed it in my head over time, I realize that that scares you. Deeply. Because you don't want to clean anything up or take any of the weight off my shoulders. You don't want any of the tragedy, chaos, or madness that lives within my being. It's always been there. But you just want the beauty behind it all.

But I am tragedy. I am chaos. I am madness.

Like Sarah Siddons, I am all these things.
But I am also beauty and grace
and lovely and refined and poised.
And I am also a muse to the artist
who wishes to capture everything I hold within
and to keep it in their memory forever.

I DESERVE MORE

I will not lose myself for any man,

even you,
the man I fell fearlessly in love with.

You were too afraid to let me love you
because you believed I deserved more.

I do deserve more.

I deserve someone
who is fearlessly in love with me.

MY LOVE

My love is not for the ill-prepared

and the weak

My love is for those ready to carry it
in their hands,
despite it being surrounded
by pounds of bricks.
My love is for those
who are willing to carry it
like a crown being carried
on a satin pillow.
My love is a jewel
and must be treated as such.

My love is an ever-growing garden
and that garden must be watered
and tended to every day
and that garden is only for those
who are willing to take on that task
and knows that by doing so,
they will get to watch me bloom constantly
and they will get to see me age
more and more beautifully as time passes by,
as my thorns begin to shrink

and become less deadly,

as my head begins to look more hopeful

and sees nothing

but light and sunshine and brightness

My love is a bird trapped in a cage

but wants to be released

and my love is only meant for those willing to release me from

the cages

that others and my anxieties

have been trying to keep me trapped in

and tried to discourage me

from spreading my wings

and taking flight into the unknown

and so my love is only for those

who want to set me free

and come with me as I explore the world.

My love is a prize,

but let me be clear:

I am NOT a trophy.

My love is the trophy.

Not my body.

Not my beauty or my looks.

Not my wealth or my physical possessions.

Not my success.

My love is the prize.
My love is who I am
and all my values
and morals
and principles
that I embody
and carry deep
within my heart and soul.
So if you want me,
you'll first have to win my love.

ROSE-COLORED GLASSES

You gaze at me

with rose-colored glasses

and that, my dear,

will ultimately be your downfall

because you see,

I am flawed,

deeply flawed,

and through the thick bushels

of rose petals

and sunshine

that I do carry and possess,

you always fail to see the thorns

scratching at your eyes,

and scarring your skin,

and causing you to slowly bleed dry.

I know I'm beautiful

and to the right set of eyes,

I am breathtaking

and I am a wonder to behold

but I am not perfect

and never will be

so take off those rose-colored glasses
and you'll see
that I am still a garden rose
even with all my thorns.

LOVE CREATES LOVE

You loved me so much

that I started loving myself ...

LEAPS OF FAITH

I've always asked others

to take leaps of faith for me

to prove their love

but I think it's time

I take a leap of faith

for myself

THE LOVE I SEEK

Maybe the love I seek

will take me my whole life to find

because maybe the love I seek

is something that only occurs

when all the stars align

Maybe the love I seek

will take me my whole life to find

because maybe the love I seek

is the one within

my heart,

my soul,

and my mind

YOU ARE EVERYTHING

You may not always love yourself

because you don't always see beauty.

But behind every imperfection there's a reason

why you are you and what makes you unique.

So embrace the good, the bad, and the ugly

and build your confidence and your talents.

Keep on working on yourself

until you strike your perfect balance.

And love your body and love your soul

because it protects you as it should –

it can stand alone and take every hit

and protects you from harm and absorbs the good.

So fuck those who don't see your worth

and say goodbye to all that negativity

because people come and go,

but self-love is worth everything.

Love your body and love your soul

because you are both the moon and the stars.

No one else can love you like you could –

no one else will ever come close to all that you are.

LEGENDARY BEAUTY

Legend has it that your face

is the face of the person

you loved most in your past life.

And since I've learned this,

I have spent more time

admiring my face,

my beauty,

and even every flaw I find,

because every bit of myself

is intentional

and beautifully and wonderfully made.

If I once loved someone so much

that it meant I got to keep

everything that makes them beautiful

and wondrous and special

in this cycle of life,

then there's no reason

why I can't love myself now.

And I want the person

who has my face in the next life

to love themselves so much

that I can feel each smile

and every beat of their heart

as they beam with joy —

I want the love I have for myself
to be felt long after I am gone.

A ROSE WITH THORNS

Have you ever heard of the phrase

"there is no rose without a thorn?"

I read that on a fortune cookie once

and in my favorite book, written in Spanish:

"No hay rosa sin espina..."

It reminds us

that despite our beauty,

both inside and out,

we have flaws and imperfections

that despite our accomplishments

and greatest achievements,

we made both small and even life-changing mistakes

along the way

and despite our fondest and dearest memories

that we hold dear to our hearts,

we carry regrets, both big and small.

And though sometimes

I wish I was like a rose without any thorns,

I might as well be a cactus

because I have flaws and imperfections galore,

I've made more mistakes than I can count

and I have my fair share of regrets,

but without my thorns

I wouldn't be who I am -

I wouldn't be the rose I have bloomed to be ...

ROMANTICIZE YOUR LIFE

I saw a post once that said
that we have to start romanticizing our own lives

and I had never read truer words ...

Because once we fall in love with our own lives
and every miniscule detail,

from the cups of coffee we drink everyday
that warms our souls and wakes our hearts
to the way our faces light up with delight
as we see our food approach our tables
at our favorite restaurants

and from the belly-aching, crying,
almost-peeing-in-your-pants laughs
you share with your friends
to the moments outside where you appreciate
all the beauty that lies in front of you

and from the way our writing is scrawled
and how you cross your t's a little too heavy
to the point where they almost rip the page
to the music that makes our hearts dance
with pure joy and abandon

and from the moments

when you're with your loved ones
and you want to pause the moment
to make it last just a few seconds longer
but instead you sigh deeply and smile
and think "this is what life is about"

to the moments where even though
reality knocked you down
and kicked you while you were still down
but you still got back up,
blood on your face, courage in your eyes,
and say confidently with a sly smile and a chuckle,
'is that all you got?'

Only then when we fall hopelessly in love
with all these moments
we will realize that there is,
and always has been,
nothing but pure romance in our lives,
even without a romantic partner ...

WHOLE

I know that I am whole, I am plenty,

for I am clothed in strength and honor.

The spaces within me

could never be empty —

I know that I am whole, I am plenty.

I am everyone, I am an amalgam of many

and I'll rejoice

because that only makes me stronger.

I know that I am whole, I am plenty,

for I am clothed in strength and honor.

FOUND WITHIN

True love is found within

because it is within ourselves

that we carry our deepest fantasies

and we dream of worlds and universes

that only we can fathom

and we carry people,

both real and imagined,

who care and love us so deeply

that it is impossible

to not be able to find the love within

FALL IN LOVE WITH YOURSELF

How about instead of

hopelessly falling in love

with others,

we fall hopelessly in love

with ourselves?

I STOPPED WAITING

I stopped breaking wishbones

and I stopped rubbing lamps

in hopes a genie would come out

and I stopped blowing the petals off dandelions

and I stopped waiting for 11:11

and I stopped whispering and praying

to the universe and the heavens

and to whatever god exists

in hopes that someone or something

was out there that could grant my wishes.

Most importantly,

I stopped waiting around

for Prince Charming

to come around and rescue me

and I stopped waiting for him to give me love –

I stopped wishing and dreaming

and decided to make my own dreams come true

and decided to give myself

the love I have always deserved ...

WHAT REMAINS OF MY HEART

What remains of my heart are pieces,

strung together

with memories, hope,

and a deep infatuation

for love.

What remains of my heart

may only be pieces

but I can live with pieces

because I know that I'm the only one

who can take the pieces

and turn my heart

into a mural,

a masterpiece -

a piece of art

so lovely and beautiful,

that it could never be lost in time.

I am always going to be the artist of my own heart.

ABOUT THE AUTHOR

Alexis M. Romo, a self-proclaimed "Flawed Artist," realized at a young age that her true passion lies in the arts, especially writing. Alexis has now published three collections of poetry and prose and has had a few pieces featured in the anthology, "Written in Protest."She graduated from the University of Arizona in 2018, studying Psychology and Philosophy, and is an advocate for mental health and education. Alexis is currently working on becoming a writing teacher so she may combine her love for writing with her love for education. She currently resides in Arizona, where she continues to indulge in her passion of creating, as well continuously fueling her never-ending curiosity.

Visit AlexisMRomo.com or her Instagram page @AlexisMRomo for more.